EL CAMINO
Spanish March

Eb Alto Saxophone 1

EL CAMINO
Spanish March

Ryan Meeboer

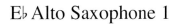

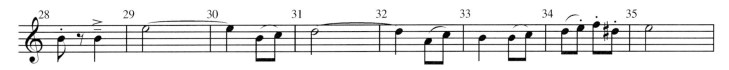

E♭ Alto Saxophone 2

EL CAMINO
Spanish March

Ryan Meeboer

EL CAMINO pg. 2

B♭ Tenor Saxophone

EL CAMINO
Spanish March

Ryan Meeboer

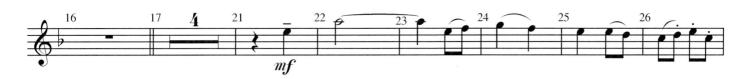

EL CAMINO
Spanish March

Eb Baritone Saxophone

Ryan Meeboer

EL CAMINO pg. 2